Praise for *Chasing the Burr*

Just the kind of debut I'd expect from Homuth—warm, nostalgic, and distinctly modern. Full of hopeful moments you can see and taste and touch—my favorite kind of poetry.

Carmen Schober, author of *After She Falls* & *Pretty Little Pieces*

+++

Here is the poet as surgeon—the one who cuts and opens to heal, with a delicacy and steadiness available only to the competent. Homuth's poems offer the nearest thing to the tactile short of the tactile itself, and his subjects emerge from his handling more textured, more whole, and more like themselves.

R. Eric Tippin, Assistant Professor of English at Palm Beach Atlantic University

+++

From the streets of Zhuhai, China, to the living spaces of any home in America, Bryn Homuth does the work of every great poet: distilling a moment into exactness and using it as a mirror to reflect our shared humanity. With observations on childhood to parenthood, a love of music to the thrill of the hunt, everything circles back on one another in **Chasing the Burr.**

Evan Kjos, Editor at PAI Consulting

+++

Bryn's poetry is refreshingly accessible, inviting us to see and experience the world differently. If you'd like to have the curtain pulled back to see the unseen of our everyday experiences, sit a while with this book.

Sara K. Davis, PhD in British Literature, Author and Teacher

Chasing the Burr

Poems

Bryn Homuth

darkly bright press

Chasing the Burr
Poems by Bryn Homuth

Catalog Number 017

ISBN: 979-8-9863904-3-7

Library of Congress Control Number: 2023930396

Publisher's Cataloging-in-Publication Data

Names: Homuth, Bryn, author.
Title: Chasing the burr : poems / Bryn Homuth.
Description: Cochiti Lake, NM: Darkly Bright Press, 2023.
Identifiers: LCCN: 2023930396 | ISBN: 979-8-9863904-3-7
Subjects: LCSH Poetry, American. | American poetry--21st century. | BISAC
POETRY / Subjects & Themes / Death, Grief, Loss| POETRY / Subjects and
Themes / Family | POETRY / Subjects and Themes / Inspirational & Religious
Classification: LCC PS3608.O68 C43 2023 | DDC 811.6--dc23

darkly bright
press & design

www.darklybrightpress.com

Table of Contents

I

oars of parenthood

page 11

II

ostinato of the thrumming heart

page 23

III

rosined scratch of dreams

page 39

IV

bread of tomorrow

page 57

V

nostalgia's backcountry

page 77

Chasing the Burr

Poems

Bryn Homuth

darkly bright press

For my wife, Jennifer
and our four children;
living poems from the Author's pen

I

oars of parenthood

Imago Dei

If the recognition could exist
as it does between motorcyclists,
how, roaring opposite one another
down a somewhere highway,
their hands will drop
into a silent, still wave,
a gesture of kinship
that does not mind
whether they will meet again,
the other's profession,
or anything, for that matter,
beyond their shared rocketing
along the road
stretched out beneath their wheels.

Oak and Acorn

The meal might have been the same
as those before it
and those yet to come
if not for the table.
Near breadth of the dining room,
finished pine end to end,
just as its chairs, it had lost its luster
once in storage, now restored
in winter light, crafted by the man
sitting at it now, his muscled hand
around a cold glass of milk,
shop-worn fingers
calloused and scarred,
as though his flesh too
wore a coating of the work.
He rests his arms
on an edge he's known
since its first shaping, like a parent
who remembers a newborn, watching
as it swelled and shrank
with heat and cold,
grandchild heads crawling beneath,
seedlings now grown
to sapling height.
Things built and things begot,
surveyed now by their Maker,
gnarled knots planed into curled shavings,
strips of blemishes swept to fall in
with the sawdust,
the finest carpentry.

Mouths To Feed

Hong Kong

I. A fisherman casts out
    into the bay, lure
    bobbing in chop
    next to wave-tossed ferries,
    an empty stringer coiled
    beneath his teetering stool.

II. Skimming a sickly film
    from a pond, she walks
    the sluggish walk of one half-submerged,
    waders mossed with more
    algae and scum
    than the net she dips
    beneath the surface.

III. Brushes and paint arranged
     like silverware,
     blank easel his empty plate,
     a sketch artist readies
     his palette.

IV. She throws her weight
    behind a steel cart
    heaped with garbage,
    her back bowed while light
    reflected by her vest
    illuminates wrappers,
    napkins, and bottles still strewn
    across the road.

V. Crouched at a pillar's base,
    masons mix patchwork cement
    in pails, flatten it
    with rusted makeshift trowels
    as if ironing shirts,
    new creases appearing
    as others are pressed.

Stigma

Blossoms reach up
out of intertwined courgette
stems, gold, splayed,
like children's hands
pressed against glass.
Inspecting them
in their raised box, I pluck one
still mostly shut
but beginning to open
to stuff, dredge, fry crisp
as dinner's amuse bouche.
Then on my fingertips
a sudden vibration,
and in alarm, a drop.
Fresh grass breaks the fall,
and from the petal purse
fly three honeybees
to alight on new stems, disappearing
into the twisted mass
as they land.
What fortune
that they did not leave,
and how I wish to be startled again
and again, as if by those living
wingbeats pulsing briefly
against my palm,
by soft, everyday tremors, to let go
as I did and see, from the confines
of wherever they commenced,
that which would pollinate.

Clementine

Her index fingernail
finds a seam

she begins to pull away
in dime-sized medallions

peelings to scatter
around the pithy

inside, hatching as if a sea turtle
breaking by caruncle its shell

out of that protective layer
that falls away, a shield

borne by branch,
transparent, here, if not for the way

the afternoon light illuminates
in dust motes encircling her chair

safeguards of the garden
shriveling to stem.

When Daughters Leave Mothers At The Airport

The hug first, always
shorter than they'd like,
the mother's hand folded
into her daughter's hair,
cheek against cheek, willing
some remnant of touch
to linger like perfume
on an empty passenger seat.

Then, the pull away, a turn
in the daughter's shoes
toward the gate. But the mother
doesn't let go, not yet,
not until she's passed
her warmth through coat and sweater
and into the heart's insulator,
where any cooling is its slowest.

Bags rustle against jackets, boarding
passes shuffle in the hands, untied
shoelaces click damp on carpet.
The mother knows only to keep
a rhythmic pat between her daughter's
shoulder blades. Their parting
is like the breaking
of a warm biscuit;
the daughter must go,
the mother must leave her,
and as the younger descends
the sloping ramp, the older takes steps
that, almost unconsciously,
would seek to follow.

Cribbage

Four pegs like relay runners
stare down a pocked track.

My father shuffles the deck
with a buzz; suits fall

from tented thumbs. I place two cards
in the crib facedown,

like the way I sleep, the way I've slept
since my first crib,

turned over by my father
when I woke.

Balance

At gymnastics, my daughter hoists herself
onto the high beam,
reddened face, sweat sticking
strands of hair to her cheeks,
teeth beginning to bare.

Rare does the lobby partition
loom between parent and child
so clear, yet cloudy;
how many are unknowingly smashed,
these barriers, like hurdles
tipped ninety degrees
before a race is ever run?

Horsebite

My uncle lifted me up
to grip the top rung
of the rusted, iron gate.
One of the mares had given birth,
and I wanted to see, clinging
still to my own birth
as I did the cold steel,
the shared condition
between us youth of our species.
Draped over the bar, I craned
for a clearer glimpse of the foal
with its shaky hooves. I didn't see
the mare shadowed
in the near stall, and provoked
by my presence she moved
with that hidden rush of speed
primed specially in the maternal adrenals
and bit my shoulder. I fell
before the pain came, but later it would,
settling as a whitened imprint
of that fierce defense. I see it
on occasion, from the corner of my eye,
a mark of the lengths mothers will go
for their newborns, that invisible armor
with which they gird their children, worn
so close to the body that its fibers intertwine
with the skin itself, sewn together
with the same needle
that passes through all of our eyes.

II

ostinato of the thrumming heart

Graveyard Jog

We passed by it once, running parallel
to the bordering stone until we came
to the archway poised at its entrance.
A primordial gateway, some ancient egress
between the living and the dead,
it was enhanced in the dark,
as though the absence of light fed
its monolithic presence. Whatever stopped us
was shined under the earth the next day
as we summoned the courage of heroes
to sprint into the cemetery.
Threadbare branches splay like guarding claws
over graves, golden boughs dew-shined,
brush our faces, while a neighboring flock of sheep
bleats with the rising sun.
There's a rusted pickup parked
near the central mausoleum
where the caretaker unloads
a rickety push mower, faded gas can,
and mulch bags from the cab.
A terranean Charon, he ferries
across the Styx as the daytime tender of souls.
I want to flip him a coin
as we lope by, a toll
to enter the rear thicket
scattered with varicose roots, bulging,
lumped stones, and flaked shavings of bark.
The path reaches a chain-link fence; we see
a family on the other side, mother, father, child,
astroll with the living. It's easier getting back,
except for one misplaced step that bruises
my heel, pulls a hiss from the ground:
a snake's head, camouflaged, coiled red
in rotted leaves.

Visits

After December dustings
cemetery sextons mark
footprinted paths to headstones,
become learned in legacies.

A Woman Nurses On The Beijing Subway

At Qianmen station, passengers battle
through turnstiles, stride
from platform through doors.
Some collapse into a seat
while straphangers find a hold
from suspended rows of grips. A lurch,
then the subway glides like an eel
through coral tunnels.
Riders sway as anemone.

A woman extends her hand
from a cluster of bodies, thin fingers cradling
crumpled *yuan*, an infant
draped over her arm, stumpy legs
dangling free, head held up by a latch
of lips to exposed breast. Her hair hangs,
a faded, dusted drape, eyes bore
through the cab, hollowing all that she sees
as she herself seems hollow.

A younger woman offers her seat—
surely the mother will sit, if only
to cradle her child—but she walks on,
sweeping her hand beneath lowered faces,
willing a head to lift, eyes to meet hers,
to restore a hope:

when the time comes to detach
her child from the food of her body,
the mother might have prepared
a bowl of rice to set in front of her daughter,
steam rising from the boiled grains.

Windowpane

Icicles grip the awning
above where he stands,
a bird feeder the only splash
of color as he stares
in its face the pane
beyond which sits his wife
in her room.

There are no chairs snow-set
for visitors outside in winter
where the low has only just begun
to walk, and the high will soon start
driver's ed.
Highs and lows like these
do not matter to him
as they once did.

How long he might stand there
nobody knows, whether they can hear
each other or prefer to leave
voices for the phone.
       How much passes through a window
       that we will never see?
The pain of glass is in its shattering,

and slow wave-wearing back to sand,
that stand-in for Time itself.
A Hand descends, gathers the grains;
they pass over Palm,
blanket the beaches of this world.
This window will come down, too,
by an errant neighborhood ball,

some architect's revision,
or in one of those instances of erosion
fully realized, 2600 Fahrenheit, maybe,
      Glass is not a crystal;
        here, there are no bonds broken.
or after wave upon wave
of sound and air and water and light

and grief have crashed against it.

On A Walkthrough Of My Wife's Childhood Home

she helps repaint the walls
and the novice historian in me stirs,
pictures her as she once ran
a hand along the first, fresh coats
just dried, walked with the tread
of discovery, raised dots and grooves
leading around the room, a kind
of Braille laid into the texture.

I try to find some trace of it now
in a pass of my fingertips, as if to touch
a faint outline, a hieroglyphic
remembrance, a cipher entombed there,
if such a cipher could exist
to unlock a person.

It must be involuntary, the encryption
of ourselves, a terminal
where the memory sits, doggedly typing,
eyes dry and heavy in the screen's glow.
If a scraper could chip
layer by layer to the base while still
preserving the rest, I would break off
and pocket those wizened flecks.

A pan of beige lies in the corner,
roller still wet, the last wall section blank.
I touch the spongy cover and rub paint
between forefinger and thumb,
as if to blend it with my skin
before it hardens.

Grey Matter

In blue scrubs, I pace
outside the OR, smile
at passing doctors, and examine
a hallway photograph of infant twins
so many times
that I feel as though I should know
their names,
or name them,
as if the charge could pass out
of the photo to me,
guardian by proximity.
Then with beckon and nod I am led
through white, clean, plain, everything
sterilized, to a seat prepared
next to my wife's head, a blue sheet blocking
her numbed, iodine-brushed belly,
waiting for a surgeon's slide
of hand to pull into life
a life.

    Before, at the ultrasound
    her belly had shined
    clear with gel like glossed ice
    as if frozen to await thawing.
    But inside: fingers, toes, spine,
    each chamber of the heart touched
    by the wand and shown as it beat
    with spindly, greyscale threads
    like newspaper print.
    We read our own, old articles there
    on the monitor, lines penned
    by our mothers and fathers
    followed by our shaky hands,
    and then noticed the baby's,
    curled, poised, as if to take up
    a pen.

I brush back my wife's hair
from her forehead and tuck it
behind her ears until, called out

from curtain, I hold my daughter
and call by name a girl
already named and called before,
in that especially long, restful sleep,
when we were all just ideas.

What a duty it is to title
the story of a person, to lay a brand
in the coals of thought
with enough heat to harm
or to apply just right a mark conceived
only after it touches, amorphous before,
not like the choices
that are black and white.

My Newborn Gets An IV

I stand at the incubator
and hold her toes, still indigo
as blood ferries oxygen
to unbound limbs.
Nurses gather at her sides
clipboards, cords, latex gloves.
They bend squeeze press turn poke.
She cries.
            They call me: *Dad.*
Frowns, no vein, and the lead nurse tells me
            the head can sometimes work.
They pinch a flap of forehead, blue
slivers like stripped wire.
I watch a needle enter her scalp, skin bulbous
like a root rupture. Another miss.
She bleeds, they dab with gauze.
            Can I call this her first wound?
They use infrared light next
as search becomes hunt.
            No danger, they say, *low glucose, routine,*
but what is she now
animal or girl
and I'm her protector, she like prey.

I pray.

Tube fast to her arm, swaddled,
to the monitor's ping we spend
our first father-daughter minutes rocking,
she to sleep,
me adrift with the oars of parenthood,
rowing out of a storm
she will never remember.

Young Twins Watch An Accordion

seated arm's length from the keyboard,
a boy and girl, patient faces alike
and different, jaws unhinged in transfixion.
The player's fingers traverse among sharp, flat,
natural; theirs twitch,
imagine a grown dexterity,
reach to walk up keys like stairs
in tireless climb of wonder,
the bellows' breath
in squeeze and stretch
like a muscle contracted
and relaxed,
like their mother's lungs from inside
the womb, a piece of their beginning
interlaid with the wood, the reeds,
the lacquered shell,
one instrument,
four hands,
symbiosis in duet.

Two Harmonicas

Zhuhai, China

The man sat wedged
against a stone wall and cracked
pavement along a city sidewalk,
his wooden cane sheathed in cloth,
curved handle leaning against a rock
like a foyer umbrella, old sheet music
piled at his feet. He drew back
and forth across a toothless mouth
as he blew through the reeds.
My friend saw him, pulled
a matching instrument from her pocket
to greet him as she could.
They soon were sharing stories
in this language: heads bent,
feet tapping, hands cupped
as if to shield fresh cigarettes.
They glowed too, together an ember
on the tip of the world, the thin trail
of their song rising
to join the atmosphere.

At 5 A. M.

my wife snugs her blanket chrysalis,
my daughter sleep-sighs
from her crib, so I try to think of something

I might do to help the world
in whatever small way a man could
bound by winter's early-hour dark.

While I wait for the thought
I flip a stove switch to light
a corner campfire, a shieldable glow,

and set to fry an egg.
Butter to pan flattens in coating melt,
then its shell split crack

as yolk and albumen dive like lovers
into a pool, pellucid, then opaque.
While feathering spatula under its edge

I notice the geometric possibility
of a perfect circle. A hunch tells me
this could be the first,

sounder even
at the atomic level than the crystal
kilogram of silicon-28
with its spherical shine,
a mathematical revelation I should share
with science and the masses.

But something about the smell,
the plating on crusty bread,
the milled crunch of sea salt and peppercorn

launches a canoe across the river
of my hunger; paddle stroke, bite. I glide
through breakfast in this way

then after extinguishing kitchen
return to my original thought and realize:
I've done it, my word the only proof.

I See My MRI

and the vertebrae gleam
silver, like nodes of moonlight,
keys of a ghostly piano
waiting to be played,
as though Beethoven's sonata
was a look inside the self,
the ostinato of the thrumming heart,
the anatomy turned inside-out. There,
the tibia and fibula that folded
to my last recital bench, cushioned
by dimples and rivulets
in front of the baby grand, its lid prop
a glossed black skin
over a cast iron frame, sinews
in the soundboard, hammer and string
viscera. I always wanted to look inside
while I played, at the smooth
padded action and steely vibrations.
These are the melodies of the protoplasm,
chiseled from the strata of composition,
assembled in score, alive.
When I sit at the keys now,
and hunch, and bend, and sway, I reenter
that old dialogue between staff and spine,
the fossils of music never extinct.

Melding

to J

My wife slices peaches,
knife slipped under the outer membrane
to peel back molten skin, models
of the sun turning on their axes,
plasmatic flesh like stars
in her fingers.
She divides one into quarters,
the blade's bump on pits,
excised, wicker-like lattices.
Red-tipped wedges drop
into the bowl; she fishes out
a piece, extends it to me,
brushing my cheek and lip.
The fruit dissolves on my tongue
while I measure flour, counter
a patched white
like early snow.
She pours like lava
the macerated peaches
into a baking dish. Once in the oven,
heat weds wet and dry,
sugar melts to syrup, caramelized
corners bubble and blend.
While the cobbler cools, we lean
against the refrigerator, its hum
at my back, my wife resting her head
on my shoulder, drawing my arms
across her front
to fit to my embrace.

III

rosined scratch of dreams

Over A Pint Of Dragon's Milk

The head smolders
as the server sets it down,
frothy, thick foam glowing
like embers, glass blown
in Smaug's charred jaws.
We wash down sliders
with draughts of molten cold,
eat to stir dormant dragons
and sing an ode to brave brewmasters,
flame-tempered fingers scalded
on mother dragon teats
like my grandfather's hands
milking cows as he sat on a bucket,
bent under a swollen udder
as open rafters leaked light
across dried blood
fissured through his fists.
I hear each dart
he squeezed out and wonder
if someday a drink will be christened
in either of our names, if we,
like the dragon, like my grandfather,
will find our place in legend.

A Shower In The Dark

The bathroom door
cracked enough to let
outside glow through
gives shape
to nozzle, soap, cloth.
Shadows on the wall.
Warmth, steam, breath, spray
like a tearing page.
After the business of the wash
with its oils, fruits, sweat, then clean,
a silhouette remains through the mist.
That person cast on the beaded wall,
hovering there, condenses
to fog on glass when the flow stops.
Solitude drips away before light floods
in; where is that glimpse of the self?
For some reason, a mirror
is not the same.

To Clear A Path

Those winter risings
to a driveway glossed
by freezing rain, my father and I
would walk out heavy,
in double-knotted boots,
layered long underwear, jeans,
sweatshirt, jacket, with wool
dome caps that exposed
only our earlobes. We'd survey first,
from the garage, then gather our tools:
scoop, shovel, and chopper.
Hack, fill, and throw,
we'd repeat, digging shallow trenches
down to bare concrete, grit and chips
like salted and peppered ground.
We'd rest, shedding a layer or two,
wiping our faces with the back of a glove
or pulling the neck of a sweatshirt over our noses,
tenting a chamber
for breath to thaw cheeks.
I'd wipe my glasses on a handful of shirt,
and the chop and toss
would resume, even though
it might begin again tomorrow.

Orange Thumb

My father crouches in packed soil,
his tennis shoes streaked black
as the earth reaches up to paint
brushstrokes curling around soles
and across laces. He pulls out a carrot;
dirt cracks and caves in
as the mouth emerges,
its ridges crusted with soil.
His first garden, the plot
bordered by bricks, tilled
into parallel rows, fenced
with thin, rabbit-stopping wire.
The carrot barely matches an index
finger, but he brings it in the house,
rinses the clay-coated ribs,
runs a thumb plow through the rows.
He pokes at it gently
as the stubby root rolls
along the hills of his palm.

Grapefruit

My father held a grapefruit,
its rind blending with his palm,
with two knives prepared
on the cloth. He rested the blade on top
before a clean split perfumed
the air with citrus, ruby halves
falling to a gentle wobble.
He outlined glistening triangles
with cuts along the pith,
rotating the bowl as he worked.
After mine, he began his own,
until we dipped into the shallow
crevasses, lifting wedges out
like spoonfuls of soup.
Juice dribbled down our chins
as we took the hollowed husks
and squeezed, remnants
of tangy nectar streaming
to pool pink in our bowls.

Plucking

Tufts of feather tugged
in quick, page-turn twists
tail to neck, patterned
and iridescent,
readying ducks for roasting.

My son stands at my side,
watches the plumage
disappear into a trash can
and by its removal the emerging
contours of breastbone, leg, and thigh,
coiled skin around the neck,
tendons and joints fit together for flight,
now food.

I tell him why we save
the wingtips and feet, how they will
fortify a stock or simmer
to glace de viande.
I show him where I'll score
the skin in diagonal cuts
to release rendering fat,
trace for him the prized oval
off the backbone: the oyster.

He runs off when, with tweezer,
I extract the pin feathers, remembering
the young drake just coming into color
that had been my first, the lesson
in the scrutiny required
to clean and steward
what I'd killed.
Then from my periphery
running in again to inspect my work, he raises
in triumph, inches from my face, dangling
from an outstretched hand, a lifeless
mouse.

I jump, shout, take his hands to wash
at the well. With instinct alone
he had gone in search of game,
to share in the hunt, to join with me
in that sacred preparation
of animal for table.

Spigot water runs clear
after the scrubbing.
Like this trickle into autumn dew,
there are things we think
we should not grasp, but instead
we have just forgotten
how to hold them.

The Duel

To the middle school student

Rusted locker rows two-high
swing, crash. There's yours,
secured by shackle, dented,
a grizzled keeper of belongings
holding your stare

as you square off like in the Old West,
bell buzzards squawking overhead,
crumpled tumbleweed tests
rolling across the hall, a slip of paper held
off at your waist like a holstered revolver.

You're a thief mid-heist
rotating the dial, ear pressed
to the plate: spin knob, skip once
in reverse, return. If only it worked
the first time, a well oiled turn
and clean pop free, but it jams.
When you finish the code, the iron
clasp whispers
You draw first,
cocked sideways,
that notorious outlaw.

Ingrained

dew film on dried red oak stacks
silhouette of doe and fawn feeding at sight's edge
white tails lift and turn with thuds into stump
silence and bark cleft by axe head's lift, pause, and plunge
I aim for the pith, split logs from a sapling, heartwood nexus

memory is not severed so cleanly
formative years entombed in the soul's crypt

I go below ground for the exhumation
descend a stone staircase, cobwebs strung along a wound
banister, a torch lit with sulfur and lime for the room
that houses the sarcophagus of recollection

Galileo must have felt this way when he first saw Saturn's rings
a tree God felled in the cosmos' vast forest
hatchet-struck to galactic timber
kindling ignites, but not all burns the same

chopped wood to fire
buried bones to the mind
planets to the infinite, black blazes
flickering throughout the universe

Moving Out

Someday you will lie on the floor
of an emptied house
in the pose of the exhausted,
a child who has flapped
the most celestial snow angel,
a replica of the Vitruvian Man.
The carpet will be clean, surrounding
walls puttied and coated anew,
and your voice, if you choose to speak,
will sweep through and rebound
magnified after addressing every
molecule of the room, even the ones
you haven't spoken to in years.
Another tenant waits
to claim this box of space, to add
to the marks of previous lives:
spilled wine, dented vents, water
stains from the upstairs bath.
You'll stare at the ceiling
and discover constellations
with the clarity of departure.
In this study,
you become your own astronomer,
detecting elusive patterns, punctures
in a black fabric, before this room
joins the others thrust up beyond
the present atmosphere, set
into perforations of memory.

(The) Rest

Musicians master it
in the elision from play
to silence
a lift of bow hair from string,
a mouthpiece drawn away from lips,
a metronomic count no one can hear,
exactness prepared
for the next note sounded.

Those included only as afterthoughts,
unnamed, passed on for roles, short
of standout effort, who linger
on the fringe of limelight, who long
to bathe in its citrus glow.

Relaxation's elusive sidekick,
more potent than the strongest drug.

Sleep may be the oldest
instance of the form,
existing even before the first mattress
with its leaves, straw, or animal skins.
It is a skill of ancient times;
when awake, we hear the rosined scratch
of dreams in the pitch of every breath,
the song of it all,
the marks of the Composer.

Lying Awake

There are arcane sounds
best discovered after dusk,
flushed like earthworms
from porous ground as the black
rain falls like to wrap
the supine body of the day.

Trains blare with rumbling railcars.
Whitecaps slosh against hulls.
Crates crack and slide in sibilating jets.
On a red-eye flight, I once heard a dog bark
or what seemed like one braying
beneath the cabin. My seat-mate stirred too,
and we shared a look, the kind that wonders,
then quickly stows away
any desire to discuss or speculate
and snugged headphones over our ears.

Tonight, it is the cadence in my wife's breath,
a fitful murmur, roll, doze, readjust,
a conversation between chemical and memory.
Without eavesdropping on the unconscious,
we could never learn these things
about ourselves. Not only old age
burns and raves as Thomas said,
but so too does the night, pacing
at my other side while I listen, angry
at how little attention it commands.

Testing Mortars

Near Fort Riley, KS

You might think your home
was a battlefield
if a bass shiver chilled the wall
when a shell thumped the ground,
old dust beaten and shaken
from the rugs.
It would not be the initial jar,
but the anticipation of those
to follow, braced against an impact
you cannot see as it lands.
If only you could fast-track sleep
by a certain closing of the eyes,
an exact stillness in the body,
a perfect cadence of inhale, exhale,
and hope it would be over
when you woke. But another
thunderous shudder,
desk lamp quaked to the floor;
rise, steady the room
piece by piece. Remember
the sigh you breathe when the tremors stop,
because you can still walk
to the front door, run a hand
along the oaken grooves, twist
the brass knob, and welcome peace
across the threshold.

Ad Lab

was my father's name
for his studio.
Walled in soundproof foam,
it was a basement room
lined as if by shelves of beakers
brimming with voice.

His microphones were suspended
from the ceiling, astral spiders
that spun speech
into silky comets.
A glass door that whispered
like an airlock, and a certain
quiet.

A quiet
like astronauts have known
in outer space,
like Orfield's anechoic chamber,
where sound is swallowed
down to organs sloshing
in a tissue dialect.

At Jupiter, the *Voyager* captured
a bass chorus reverberating
from the planet's fathomless chest.
Stare into the Great Red Spot, and there
are the same cobwebs,
remnants of sound that cling
even after being brushed away.

Underwater Thoroughfares

Gulls rest on the tip
of submerged dock posts
while a mallard's low feeder chuckle
splits the usual sopranos on the wing.
I reach for the bait bucket,
sweep my hand through
while streamlined bodies dart above
and below my finger arches, trap one
between cupped palm and wall,
then weave the hook up
through the tiny lower jaw, out
the top of its head. Over pontoon's prow,
I rinse minnow and earthworm grime
from hook-bitten hands.

My father once wondered to me:
What if you could levitate
all the fish in a lake, if only for a moment?
To see them, scale luster
and lengths immobilized, I would wonder
which were to be caught and
which would swim in aimless float
until, buoyancy lost, fins limp,
they'd sink to marlstone.

Paved with pebble and silt, obscured
by muck, weed tips wave wispy,
wraithlike, over the lake's highway.
With the road-weariness, it's no surprise
at the sneer in underbit bass lips
or a pike's frenzied maw.
What is their heaven,
but an unsuspecting pass through sky,
bones filleted away
from the fisherman's prize? The lake itself
is destined to be rich farmland,
once the bed is laid bare,
the width of those aquatic roads a plan
for planting uniform rows,
soil of unmatched fertility,
crops in abundance.

Under The Tree

Highway 108, Pelican Rapids, MN

For Lucas

Geyser-like, its limbs flow
out from the base fountaining
over one another, yet never touch
ground as a weeping willow might.
Returns to the earth require
those tears.

I've seen it only by photograph, but I know
how I'll visit: Saturday, in summer,
I'll park and walk in, sit back to trunk
and look up through the canopy.

It is the bouquet your bride would have held,
a pianist's hand across the ivory clouds.
Then will begin the rubber-runs in passing tires,
wind arpeggiating up leaves to octaves untouched,
notes struck by the accompanying left hand
of the wild, a piece with no name.
The roots record it in topsoil,
a song entrusted to their keeping
kept on repeat, ceaseless
adagietto strains, audible,
light-giving.

IV

bread of tomorrow

You Would Have Been A Blacksmith

my optometrist tells me,
had you been born in the Middle Ages.
Better with one here, or two?

Phoropter's click
seems to clang—a version
of me, before and without
the corrective lens,
hammers misshapen metal,
sparks shower like geysers,
embers die in the dirt.

Brow sweat never dry,
face streaked with soot, he flexes
burn-scarred hands, hunches
before the forge. Each turn
on the anvil fashions
an edge still blurred, known
only by its heft, shape, and glow.
Plunge into slack tub, submerge,
smoke of rapid cool, out again,
its sheen like the gloss of fresh ink.

Were I to send this man a letter,
I would compose it in the old way:
with a wisp of quill, faint scratches
against parchment,
in measured dips to inkwell.
I would hope he could read
and write as large
as the page would allow.

I would describe to him
my wife and my children's faces, the rising
and setting sun, acquaint him
with the moon.

Even though I would not expect
a reply, I would ask what projects
are in his queue: prisoner's irons,
horseshoes, armor
and weapons of war.

I would look out the window
and try to think of more to say,
before finally signing
our shared name,
my writing arm sprawled
across the drying script,
lifted away, rotated,
a helix of black
traced over my veins.

Dream

The first morning of a new year,
I hear a knock against the teak
of sleep and open it to a box
just beyond the threshold.

Inside, I find a couple
riding a tandem bike
down an early autumn road,
tires spinning through leaves
kicked up and shredded
by the spokes, a picnic wrapped
in their front basket. They left
their home with the hope
of getting lost,
if only for an afternoon,
pedaling for a trail
worn by rainfall and wind
into the forest of privacy.
Nobody knows they have arrived there,
shaded under a lush elm, eating
as light drips through the canopy
to oil the ground.

I set the bloodhound
of my pen to their route,
barely keeping stride
as his nose skims asphalt,
then earth
and grass,
but something moves me
to leash him, before we arrive,
when their attentions have turned
fully from the world
and to each other,
and drag him back
through the brush to preserve
some part of their sanctuary.

The First Bread

Without a recipe propped
next to flouring board
or the precision of measurements,
it was simply hand-milled grain
mixed with oil, water,
rolled flat and fed
toward a flame.
Who can guess
how many attempts?
The browned, amorphous edge
that became *tortilla, naan,*
lavash, cake, pita, matzah,
and the blackened, failed crusts
that made their names.

The First Surfer

It must have begun with a stare
into the crashing water, different eyes
than any who looked out
on the waves before, a version of those
who scanned up a cragged rock face
before fitting a toe to a horseshoe crevice,
drying palms, straining for a handhold.
Or those who set bladed feet
atop a powdered peak, pointed
toward the downslope as a slow glide
accelerated into a fall.
That's how it must have been
that day on a somewhere beach,
the slip of cool grit between toes
not satisfying enough, the breeze
seeming to quicken in gust,
beckoning from shore's edge.

With driftwood worn smooth
by tidal lapping, musty, slivered
in urchin spines, a belly-down paddle
through the shallows; hammerheads below
slash through the deep.
After a breath of quiet,
a water column rises
under the makeshift board.
The rider stands, balances; sunken
instinct surfaces. A seismic churn
sweeps into surf's curled mouth,
and breaches an unending
tunnel, one others will enter,
chisels in hand, to chip away
the eddying swirls that vanish
as soon as they are carved.

Awaiting The First Surgery

The patient writhed
awake, a root tight
between the teeth,
boa-like grip to
whatever was nearest:
another's fingers,
a sapling limb, or
a desperate clawing
to dig up
anesthesia
before it ever had a name.

Drop Anchor

The smaller are most often stored on deck,
algae-caked, rusty, covered in coiled
rope before the skipper untangles, torques
metal tethering beneath the oily

surface. Line pulled taut, like boat and lake floor
wrenched away in a stalemate tug-of-war,
braiding between stretched nearly to an
audible flex. Others will jettison

from a cavity in the ship's keel, pitch,
plunge down, lodge in sand, rock, unseen debris
not yet swallowed by Marianas Trench.
Should one dislodge, lie too light, if it be

kedge or plow, the vessel could station crew
in a place they may have passed straight through.

Back Burner Ballade

sockeye scored, salted
black peppercorn grind
skin-down to hot oil
garlic head's clove-crack
knife flat, press, sliver-slice, chop
lemon roll by palm
zested like a citrus polish brush
buffing a shoe

Water slosh. Burner, high.

rip of sweet corn shucked
zucchini shaved gossamery
over mandoline
mirepoix minced, mosaic
whisk against bowl
spatula scrape
meringue mounds
still, stiffen

Hiss. Boil brink.

ribeye rest, crosshatched
grill sizzle tapers
herb butter basted
rosemary and thyme walnuts tossed, toast
cold, crunch-cut romaine
Roquefort dress, drizzle
bacon fat rendered
crackles, constricts

Lid lift. Glop, glop.

Pinot noir, auger twist,
twist, cork hoots free
like a casted lure breaks the surface
a stream of wine glugs into pour

A watched pot eventually boils.

Nightcap

I've invited Sleep out
for a drink, but here I am
sitting alone.

I look at my watch, and see
Sleep is late, as usual
whenever we've made a plan.

Always an advocate
for the spontaneous
Sleep has no problem

making impromptu visits
but something about a plan,
a selected time, puts him off.

Tonight, I wish he and I
had arrived together,
finishing our tall beers

at the same time,
his light,
mine dark

(I'm forever asking Sleep
to try something dark),
tab in his fist

before I can think
to pay, a practice to which
I've grown accustomed.

Ants

I covered nineteen
or some other number
of them when I set the first trap
down, a white-walled room
with two doors, the kind, armed
with human sensibility,
one might suspect for its likeness
to an asylum or horrific hospital

but ants, for all their fabled
strength, follow sugar's allure
with reckless abandon
and boulder-haul like hoarders
before a storm. Few creatures look
so uniform from our vantage point,
the trail like clones off an assembly line

but were I an ant, I'm sure,
down on that microscopic plane, I would know
that that is Bill from the mound next door,
always piloting his drone from the back patio,
or Dave on the other side
who likes to get his mail slippered,
late in the day, as evening engulfs dusk.

Even in our suburban formicaries,
pheromone trails weave through
and out the neighborhood.
They call to me now
as, from under the trim, worker
after worker, unsuspecting,
in dutiful obedience to instinct,
collects and returns to the nest
poison that cripples the colony.

Fantasy Football

The name might call to mind
a contest between two teams
of some fictional race,
as though dwarves or elves aligned
toe-to-toe on a snow-speckled field
in a land not our own.

Wouldn't a wizard be under center,
with his command of the material world,
an incantation or wave of wand
to send pigskin into outstretched hands?

How alike a book, the practice
allowing one to inhabit a far-off
gridiron as a player would, to crouch
and dig knuckles into grass or turf,
to growl fog through a facemark,
to crunch pad against pad, a battle
where the only arms
hang from the collar.

But this, after all, is fantasy, and detachment
means only a click of a mouse,
until another rung appears
on technology's ladder, a simulator,
a vicarious leap beyond
that of mere observation,
where the magic of the score becomes
palpable, their touchdowns your triumph,
their bruises fresh, your own
muscles tender and sore.

Wisdom Teeth

Dentist's finger-fishhook
in my cheek, I look solely
upward, a flounder at market.
An inspecting pick lifts out, in,
a mine where the headless headlamp
illuminates cavities; the plaque
on the wall reads: D.D.S.

An x-ray shows four
in tooth-hibernation, grisly
rarities at my age.
They don't need to come out, I learn,
but the pain worsens with time,
the usual sutures, swelling, soreness,
and byproducts not disclosed:
dormant knowledge cast in enamel,
molten, sweating eruption.

How many of the greats
endured such a jaw-ache?
Solomon listening
to claims over a child,
Carver squinting
at a peanut through eyepiece,
Einstein examining
a crowded blackboard,
finger-twirling chalk.

Maybe it is the real reason
for that pensive rubbing of the chin.

No more chewing
on this idea, I tell myself as I leave,
not the whos, the whats,
the whens, the wheres,
or even the whys.

Nail Biter's Relapse

Mine always come while writing,
the first victim usually the index
finger stationed as it is
at the helm of the pencil,
responsible, as a leader should be,
for the hand's other digits.
How fortunate I am,
that before the nail is rent
across the cuticle,
my wife hands me a clipper
to detach before it bleeds,
ragged, uneven, and ugly,
that which I have started
to tear away.
My grandmother once offered me
fifty dollars to quit, an incentive
I feel uncomfortable ever redeeming
despite the growth and regrowth
that may cover past marrings.
The phantom bill appears like a tattoo
wrapped around palm
and back of my hand
whenever I look
at it, Grant's resolute countenance,
a look borne from warring
halves, internal struggle,
the straight-lip stare that I am sure
she chose on purpose.

Pipe, Wood

Pinch from tobacco tin,
ribbons like paper shreds
long-burning,
an inglenook for gnats
orbiting the workshop's single bulb.

Pack, bowl fill, scratch a match
orange, pull, puff like a pitch warble:
sharp—flat—sharp—
waved off by conductor.
A billow-chord sounds from my mouth.

We lift a half-finished table
upside down, fit stretcher to trestles
in mortise and tenon,
sand paper grit fine, orbital buzz tuning
sawdust to spent smoke.
Hum flickers low, then out.

Peace of exhale and night,
voices of trees dead and alive sing
in the rafters, and black cherry attuned
to itself awaits a finish:
pipe-gurgle faint
like a timpani's roll,
a note-sheen
bright, fragrant, built.

Subzero Hunt

I trace a boot-stamp byway
through the tree line and
cabin lights dwindle to thin haze
before a headlamp is my only guide,
its beam whetting edges of muddled tracks
labyrinthine in aimless wind,
some hoof, some heel, some overlaid,
some touched by wolf paw's tireless tread

I almost hear one when I stop
a distant howl, a cracking twig,
a low, serrated growl
roiling in dawn's starved belly,
but there is only heartbeat and hum

squirrels scale bark, mice nose out
from brush, I whisper wild breath

up the stand to chair, rifle snug to shoulder

there is a pull to the immobile
that the cold cannot ignore,
inhabiting stowed reserves of warmth
beneath flesh

so begins my meld
with the backdrop of the land, another
fallen log, branch sheathed in frost,
acorn or apple core cratered in snow

when the deer bed down with the day
I start a noiseless descent
and think back to that morning wait,
the patience of the wolf,
if I am predator, or prey,
and if a piece of me remains,
never to thaw,
frozen to the roost.

Midnight Michelangelos

Snowplows chisel impassable streets
a path the blizzard-imprisoned plod
while flakes, torn, shredded, fall in sheets.

A driver awakens, night-morning greets;
his helm a blade two-mouthed and broad,
the snowplow's chisel through drift-dammed streets

tills lanes free, but, bittersweet,
hungry traffic grinds like a bone being gnawed
the flakes, torn, shredded, falling in sheets.

This, the plow's food, as a combine its wheat
chunked and dug up like unbroken sod
fuels its chisel through stonewalled streets.

Unsatisfied, the plow gobbles its meat
nibbling away at winter's facade
which flakes, torn, shredded, fallen in sheets.

Citizens sleep while the process repeats,
unnoticed art of a sculpturing squad
with their snowplow chisels in the streets
flaking the torn, shredded, fallen sheets.

North Dakota Fable

The auger's toothed helix
oscillates in snow blower's mouth,
faster as I nudge the lever
to turtle then rabbit,
the same as Aesop's adversaries

but what would they have done with snow?
The books show a clear, winding trail,
at least one tree for the rabbit's pause.

Consider a starting line drawn
across ice, foot-high drifts lining
and spilling into the raceway.
Traction would be problematic,
no explosive sprinter's burst
off the block, but the lead
would still be the rabbit's.
There would be less scenery
for the green-skinned trailer,
but would he have the leisure
to observe? Down at his ground
skimming sight, pebbles loom
like boulders.

My concern is that the moral
would be overturned, rabbit robbed
of his customary nap by subzero chills,
kept awake to stumble across the finish
hardly feeling the victor, instead
wishing for an inside-out warming
like a sip of steaming broth might give.
Perhaps the turtle's mother
would have something prepared
despite her hatchling's second place finish,
a consolatory reptilian stew
to spoon past his beaked lip.
As the engine warms to a low hum,
I push the lever into the turtle slot,
wheel out into powder
that the swiveling chute blows sideways;
new flakes fall,
flecking the pavement wake.

Evening Harvest

A combine headlight filters
through the underbrush
of night, a lighthouse
for the land-locked, its beam
a beacon for the field,
for the work to be done there:
slow claw of the plow,
seeding, watering.

Today, though, harvest heaves open
the heavy cellar door
of the dark, highway travelers
oblivious, wearing blinders
of a twilit journey
without glance toward the planted
acres, drafty barns, the homes
where laborers sleep.

This farmer is awake,
churning through crop, rousing himself
with each wheel turn
as he rouses the ground
at the hour when even the land
seems to close its earthen eyes.
Here begins the bread of tomorrow.

If we were wayfarers of a buried age,
there would be no way to know
the other was there. Even yards apart,
the swish of his scythe
or the brush of his winnowing fork
would have sounded like the prairie wind
passing over my ears.

V

nostalgia's backcountry

Avogadro At The Pond

Rink a shared stone,
smiths whet mettle
in pursuit of the puck,
cracks like hammer strikes
on the vulcanized rubber
chock against the boards.

Carpenters too, their skates
routers channeling through wood,
a design drawn, redrawn,
elaborated upon,
rivaling Picasso's *Ma Jolie*.

Like a boomerang,
I once threw a hockey stick
in childhood, at my brother
during a driveway pickup game.
It slashed through his cheek
between two moles, division
stitched in the dermis;
the memory itself
banks and whips back
toward my outstretched hand,
whirring through the vaporous mols
of regret.

Breath plumes grey
against the black sky.
Strides shorten, slow.
Sharp stops strew
crystalline shavings. Goals
in single, chainlink chimes.

Among resurfacers, sandpaper
knows few equals. With the grit
that is necessary, firm friction applied,
layers buff away,
cake the hands,
pile in dust.

Ice, however, is the smoother's jewel;
washed, shaved, rewatered
to freeze together the old and the new,
an alloy of fresh skin and scars.

Aix Sponsa

A myrtle crest stitched
to a yellow cuff dovetails
to a sunrise beak,
the drake's plumage pressed
and steamed as he flies
at first light
behind Dawn's doors.
I watch him,
as would any wedding guest,
from the river bank,
groom's side, I suppose,
my pew a pail flipped,
tucked in tall grass.
Wind strums a leaf-harp
with the river-aisle prepared.
They sing their own processional,
the wood ducks, of wingbeat
and whistle, announcing themselves
in flocks matrimonial.
Listen as they join the chorus
of bridegrooms
in churches, farms, fields,
aboard boats,
along lakeshores and beaches,
all choirs
in the Bridegroom's sanctuaries.

As Slow As Possible

Based on the piece by John Cage

Patience has no place
in the church,
not anymore, not at the organ
built for six centuries'
undertaking, pipe and pedal
imbued with resilient alloy.
Encased in a wall of glass,
its abyssal groan shakes
dust from the air
into pollutant wisps
of immortality. To breathe them
might vault a mind forward
to the dream
of a Methuselanic Age;
a congregated host
of centenarians clasp their hands
around worn, wrinkled Bible pages,
heads greyed and white.
The blind will be lucky
if the condition still exists
while those chosen approach
the throne of a bench,
no nervous knuckle rubs
on pew as the weights are removed,
just the steady reverberation
in the ear
never quieted.
Outside, a schoolboy stoops
to pick a rock in the courtyard.
A young woman's hurried heel
pops against cobblestone.
Gardener shears click.
A nun kneels in prayer.
A concert the first of its kind,
listeners engrossed
not by beginning, nor middle,
nor end, not by voice or string,

but by the stoppage of a line
long as Hapsburg,
an acoustic dynasty.
There are those who will file out
as dutifully as they arrived,
shielding their eyes
from a harsh light,
walking a new epoch,
while others inside remain
seated, wondering at the things that endure,
the heaviness of dying
tones settling into their feet
for minutes, then hours,
until they begin to question
how they'll ever leave.

The Snapping Turtle

I came upon him
a late May morning
crossing the road like a knight
returning from battle,
black shell-shield
spattered with moss
slung on his back,
a grimace in his beak-lip.
He dragged each leg
as if probing a minefield
or inching under barbed wire,
tubercles a short-spiked carapace
gouged, bitten, banged like armor
of a young blacksmith's fashioning.
I wondered if he once fought
side by side with Bishop's warrior fish
as he moved with that fabled
reptilian patience on into roadside brush.
He went, I knew then,
to meet his brother
at a secluded lake
where a fallen tamarack trunk
stretches out over the water, a sanctuary
to sun his blood warm. Nearby
the fish nibbles mayflies; between them,
the veterans' silence
that expects nothing
and is content
with one another's company.

The Sky Underground

Wader-slogging
through submerged stubble,
we haul netted packs
plump with goose guises
and mallard mannequins
to display in the corn's store window.

A migrator's shelter,
pond pooled by storm, harbored
heads of black and green.
We saw them yesterday from the road
preen and pasture,
ready for a southward soar.

The bank recedes already
as the waterfowl bivouac
prepares to break camp,
its muddy fringe brushing dried soil,
twilit, as though Earth's terminator
cast the spot in two-toned shadow.

Now, stars reflect on halcyon
water like diamonds veined in coal,
an immeasurable, galactic gorge
sloping to a true vanishing point.
The illusory precipice dares me over
and below, a simultaneous tumble

to core and cosmos; one step—
a mucky stalk-squelch, ripple,
distorts the glinting mine.
With the unwind and drop of each decoy,
I pass my hand through the nebulous
jewels and become
a version of Aesop's dog,
the wealth he carried and tasted
that did not satisfy
at the zenith
and nadir of himself,
distant as the sky underground.

After Blizzards

when whipping white sidewinders
snake no more through intersections,
when store windows darken
and lit frames of billboards dissolve
into black sky

only the day's snowfall remains
in the street, some heaped,
some packed by tire tread, a sculpture
in flux like clay thrown and shaped
and thrown again, a carving
cut, whittled, rough-hewn from winter.

Muscling through city avenues,
snowplows emerge like bears
in walking hibernation, frost creatures
that tunnel through compacted drifts.
These plowmen, unseen
agents of dream hours, leave
only ice-etched wakes.
Those stirred may hear the blades
crunch against curbs and join
faint whispers of the evening:
a jet turbine's receding drone,
an ambulance's tapering siren.

Morning traffic comes
to clog the cleared lanes,
the work remembered only by
and under
the streetlamps' insomniac gazes.

Norwegian Blood

My daughter follows
from shelf to cart
carrots, corn, then *krumkake*
and *lefse*—that, we used to make ourselves,
thin dough spread on a circular griddle,
turning stick feathered underneath,
lifted, lowered, rotated slowly in the fingers to unfold
        as if braiding hair
        or fastening a small button
a soft crust blotched in brown,
like skin as it ages.

At the butcher I choose a ham
and meatball mince while my mother
eyes *lutefisk. Should we?* she asks.
Only you and I would eat it now.

I see the fish as it used to be,
salted by my grandmother's hand,
my grandfather later
as he would recline from table,
declare it *good lutefisk*, savoring the full,
hooted "u" as it lingered in his mouth.

I slice into it at Christmas dinner,
roll it out of oven in a butter bath
while my mother does the same.

It finds us all, tradition,
as a fish might: by chance, slippery,
scaled, passing beneath
things more readily observed.
Without a tight grip, a landing
by spear, by hook,
or by well-timed net,
it can, and will, tail-flip free.

Bivalves

For my grandmother Pearl

I.
A boy nicknamed
Polar Bear,
pen pal to summer,
is a boy
you would expect
knows wind chill
is cold's true augur
and shoveling
is only one part snow
and other parts
drive, loosen,
spiderweb, shatter,
scoop, heave.
He has never braced
for a hurricane
or shucked oysters
on an estuary pier,
knife finding hinge,
twist and pry,
muscle severs,
shell's opening,
meat and pearl.

II.
My mother waited
for the coroner
as a blizzard howled
and tore down
deserted streets.
She lifted her mother
onto gurney,
into a body bag,
and the world became
a set of things
halved, raw, and open:
the unzipped bag,
vehicle doors, hearts
bivalves to be closed,
with jewels to return.
The storm blinded,
netted, and rent the air;
you would expect
she knew those things,
another child of the north
trying to make winter
a comforting companion.

Purple Heart

At the Fourth of July parade
slumped in a fold-up chair,
cowboy hat low over thick eyebrows
hiding the jungle in his eyes,
he tapped his boot against a crack
in the pavement
and didn't stand for the flag.

The next day at his farm,
he pats the back of his strongest mare,
she neighs, trots away,
splits clods of manure and dirt.

He shakes a stiff leg,
thumbs a round scar on his thigh
through dusty jeans, and turns
to warm his face on the morning.

Spring Back

My father steadied himself
against the kitchen counter
with his good arm,
fingers pressed white against marble,
face darkening
as he forced labored breath
from between clenched teeth.
He slid the other arm from its sling,
the limb hanging down
like a tentacle,
pink and yellow-purple, then rocked it
as the doctor recommended,
a loose pendulum
tracing circles, like a watch
as its time is set. At a break
he looked at the tissue crossed
by stitches, a shoulder once taut
with round-muscle bulge
that my brother and I envied
when we would flex in the mirror,
seeing what our bodies might become.
In that same arm, with its shrunken,
elastic skin, we saw for a moment
every leaf raked, post driven,
rock loaded. We saw the arms that raised us
to saddle the shoulders
and look out over the tops of crowds,
then gently pinched our biceps,
pulled, released,
and understood
that we are the opposite of clocks
which, despite being advanced
or returned by one hour
in the summer and autumn,
can, by their mechanism,
return perpetually
to what they were before.

The Thoughts That Do Not Return

are not always those one might expect,
the wedding aisle, a firstborn's swaddle,
but instead, a recipe: mix, leaven, roll, slice
full pans of straw-brown swirls.
A clock becomes memory's barometer.
Arrange the numbers,
fit the hands, hang it on the wall
as long as it will stay. How many of us
know the time of our births,
the very fixture of the hands,
one short, one long, two arrows
frozen mid-flight to a target
out of range like the hands
that led us from fluid and womb?
She measures flour, eggs, and butter
while her daughter measures
her, takes stock, catalogues
the mind's pantry, that prominent shelf
where her mother, stored, leaks slowly
from a puncture none can patch.

Muscle Memory

Our polka band plays a waltz,
bass thumps a three count,
accordion eases open,
and a couple stands
from the audience. The husband,
with thinning grey hair,
spotted wrists and forearms,
bows to his wife, her curtsy
in flowered dress more tenuous
than it used to be, and they're off,
stepping in time, tracing a line
through folding chairs.
I imagine them like this at twenty,
in a ballroom with tiled floors
shined to reflect the dancers
like a grove of trees mirrored
in a glassy lake, as though they danced
both above and below ground,
on one side of their lives
and today, the other.

If An Animal Dies On The Roadside
And No One Sees It

A common motorist's encounter,
the deer looked
freshly hit, only just removed
from its last bound over guardrail,
collapsing into that shallow trough
next to windblown trash bags
and yesterday's cardboard box.
I passed it every day for weeks,
wondering why a State Trooper
or the DOT hadn't disposed
of the noble carcass, why no coyotes
or vultures sought a meal, scavengers
of the night. Each morning its auburn
hide dulled as the grass grew, stalled,
then began to brown. Winter's mortician
tried its best to draw a sheet
over the animal, a hospital courtesy,
but no gurney of the wild came,
and frost and thaw dueled
over the rites: bury, exhume, bury beyond
the line of convenience for retrieval
as it was. There was a morning I saw
its antlers had been removed, regal
points that had poked through the snow
reminding where it lay
gone, sawed off under cover.
I like to think they found
a use, at least as a handle, a cabin furnishing,
or even a good dog's bone. Still
its unblinking eyes remained, until, without
warning, they did not. Like a chalk outline
the ground held its imprint, grass that eventually
grew longer, greener, straighter,
a temporary monument for the resident
voles, cottontails, and meadowlarks
that might pay homage
to fallen royalty among them
before the next ditch mowing.

Poem For A Man Near Death

Frame, mattress, and spring,
his bed is not yet a deathbed, re-made
each morning hoping to turn back
sheet, forming a triangle like a boy
folds paper airplanes at a desk.

He walks slower now, shuffles, curled
as though his body gathers back
into itself, neck drawing from back,
back from legs, legs drawn
by the bone-magnet in the ground.
It begins to pull at his heels.

Could it be a gift, this preparation,
a chance to become Death's reconnoiter?
See him as a farmer over horizon's hill,
his sickle-shadow less menacing
as it cuts wheat to bake
an imperishable bread.

Ribbon Bound

In care center lobby
a woman in wheelchair
hunches from her parked position
at a television she may not hear.
One foot has edged off its pedal,
shoe nosing carpet as she clutches
a baby doll in her arms.
She sways in her seat
the way she coaxed her own child
to sleep, and closes her eyes.
Behind them, in the private
film room of her thoughts,
reels line shelves like spools of ribbon,
some missing, some piled to ceiling.
She selects one, loads projector,
its whirring click like shuffled cards
switching on. This dark room
down a dark hall
in a dark building
emits a lens light refracted
through doll's countenance.
She wakes, finger-combs
ribbon-tied hair, and searches
its plastic optimism for the infinitesimal,
illuminate thread she can follow back
because a room that dark
must be difficult to find.

The Unfinished

Schubert's 8th in B minor floats
in two movements, down the channel
of a violin string on the fragile raft
of the incomplete
as it's buoyed again.

Its waterlogged planks splinter and sag
beneath ages of cargo:
Gaudi's *Sagrada Familia*, towers
spearing into clouds,
Chaucer's nameless pilgrims on horseback,
hoof-tracks erased
as they're clopped into dirt,
or Da Vinci's *Gran Cavallo*
as it crumbles, arrow-gouged legs mid-stride.

Each is two works in one,
the piece that is
and the piece that is not.

At symphony's close, I soak in stillness,
an end not quite an end,
a feeling I recall
from a drive through Chinese cities,
the roads lined with skyscraper sketches
fenced by bamboo scaffolding.

At a distance, those trellises
were blank ledger lines
on staff paper, the spaces unfilled
where no notes will find their rest.

Claw Back
for Tim

We woke to your sobs
muffled against the tent,
a sound our subconsciouses knew
was not of the forest,
and listened through the dark.
Even now, I still wonder what it was:
a terror, a dream, a fleeting thought
or remembrance, the nocturnal sort
that breaks open cerebral coolers
unsecured, rummages through
and feeds on the past.
It sent you tearing open the zipper
and stumbling out into gnats
and midnight. We followed
not knowing how to chase away
the swarms inside and outside
your head as they bit
and you clawed at them, then sank
into a soggy meadow and held you,
hoping it would pass.
If we'd known then,
how could we have returned to camp
and simply slept
given a food-conditioned bear
huffed and moaned in the wilderness
of your mind, no spray of man
potent enough to drive it back,
no caliber of a virulence to fell the beast.
Instead of dwelling on it—the mauling—
I turn instead to a hike
through nostalgia's backcountry
with its dens and caves,
the one in which I hope to find you,
and by the clapping of my hands
or a shout, wake you
from this long, long hibernation.

The Freight Of Leaves

Wind swells and ebbs in the leaves
like tide on sand, passing through
fronds rustled like a wave's crash
against rocky shoreline, skeletonized veins
chilled almost blue, like the oceans that
stretch beyond window frames,
the foam, the shimmer, the refracted light
glazing a coral shelf where clownfish
part poison tentacles, morays
slip among sunken alcoves, and rays' barbed tails
stir their sandy cloaks. Fathoms down, anglerfish
glow like excavator headlamps, whales
lounge in buoyant rest, baleened beasts
with blowholes sighed shut. Dive,
as they dive, into a tree's gathered vegetation,
phyllospheres' cytoplasmic seas,
mitochondria floating,
ribosomes on atomic vessels
and chloroplast ports in solar-paneled harbors
unloading their green crates.

She Made Us Soup

For Elizabeth

She was dying, and she made us
soup, *Vichyssoise*, silk-spoken
pale spoonfuls sipped
cool, not cold.

The pot had been left outside,
snow-swaddled just beyond
the back threshold
because it could be, the rest

of the meal filling the fridge
or counter-strewn.
We brought it in after the salad,
endive's crunch fading

in our mouths,
and ladled into rose-etched china
a color that was like
her color, blanched

as, the night before, the leeks
had been: scrubbed,
leaf to root,
sliced, scooped, and sautéed
to feed healthy bodies
as her own starved.

Forgive me,
it was so delicious
that I have almost forgotten
the other courses

and would prefer to, fully, now,
as though a dozen of us
had gathered only for her
soup, and to sit beyond

the point where even night
has turned in,
across from her at table, there—
head bowed, hunched,
wrapped in a blanket—knowing
that we would leave hungry.

The Lady Who Lives Upstairs

brews coffee, a stout, afternoon pot
to sip watching grove's shadow,
pine and maple stick-forts, the RV left
split by tree for two decades.

Pour, pot-gurgle faint, she turns
to window opposite, seeing
the storage shed braced by post,
leaning horse barn beside, loft
spread in weathered hay,
harnesses hanging dust-stiff.

Steam stencils cabinets inside,
distant plow carts like rusted
mirage in the vapor. *Mom,*
do you want a cup?

Her mother, in a mix of whispers
and mutters, says
Shouldn't we brew a big pot
in case the men want some?

The lady who lives upstairs remembers
when the men would come in from the fields.
She's lived here before.
She was born here.
Sure. You can make a big pot.

The Handkerchief

A crumpled tissue
for dabbing spit
at the corners of his mouth
hung open like a fish's

he fumbles to stuff it
in the breast pocket of a shirt
he's not wearing
but used to wear
when he could dress himself.

His hand lifts, drags down a plain
white tee, drops through a phantom
pocket to his lap, a cycle like water
as it gathers in a cloud,
falls,
stills,
then evaporates.

Much of what is worn
is not removed so easily
as clothes unbuttoned, shed,
washed to strip away
grease streaks or oil smears.

He could imagine his chair
was a shop-stool
drawn to the hood
of a gutted Model A,
his television an engine
leaky, frail,
the remote control a wrench,
fingers miming a bolt-tighten twist
that, given the cold, he'd pause
only to wipe a runny nose.

Bandaging

My grandmother rolls
the hem of her shirt
as she would a piece of lefse,
curling it into a tight cylinder,
exposing her mole-dotted stomach,
a pale, wrinkled mound,
skin hanging in loose piles
collected at her waist.
My mother wears rubber gloves
as she pulls away a moistened strip
of pus-yellowed bandage
like old wallpaper steamed loose,
pipes a cleaning solution
over the bloodied gouge.
The incision seems etched,
edges gray with healthy tissue
spreading to cover pink flesh.
She pats it dry with a towel;
my grandmother winces
at the dry scratch of gauze
fitted, cut and pressed
thin and white
like strands
of her hair. When my mother
places a new dressing,
she smoothes the corners,
presses fabric flush to seal it.
After she's finished,
my mother leaves her hand
on the rising and falling belly,
leaning forward
as though she might lay her head
in the space between wound and navel,
a gentle press of the ear,
listening to sounds of her home.

The Empty Field Game
Baltimore, April 29, 2015

If America's pastime could continue
past time, after the reign of noise and city,
when most have retreated
to hidden places of the world,
this game would be a mirror to that future—
crack of ash against ball,
smack of fist and leather
ghosting through a phantom crowd
that does not stretch its arms
to soften a home run's flight
or shout a thousand cheers
like a rush of water.

Were entertainment to wait
out the apocalypse,
this is the sanctuary to where
it might steal away, the diamond
with the hardness of its underground twin,
choked in but lustrous still, gleaming
if only for those who discover it.

Spiked cleats scratch and gouge
base paths like a pickaxe swung
again and again against a vein
of coal, athlete a miner with no witness
to his craft, only the glove
of the dark clamped loosely
across his mouth as if to stifle a scream,
when all that can be mustered
is a wheeze, a cough, a sputter,
anything that might clear the dust
from his slowly filling lungs.

Chasing The Burr

From an oak-crown roost
the barn owl dropped
like a hush
to a grass glide, a blade
over air, unsheathed
wing tips honed
on wood's whetstones.

In the stroke of its flight
I felt, from the edge
of a meadow on a cross
of fallen logs, the field mouse
inside me quiver, nose,
become stone
in the eyes' Medusian fix.

A stare with the fullness of time
bound between it and me
like a rabbit
cutting through cattails
then passed me over.

Few seconds I have lived
were at once so blunt
and became so diurnal
opposite the nighttime predator.

It nests now in my thoughts'
abandoned barn,
ghosting in and out,
a rafter-wraith bobbing its head
like a knob in moon
and rotted beams, alit
at a broken window,
its hooked beak a burr
from shadow into gleam.

About the Poet

Bryn Homuth grew up in Fargo, North Dakota and earned his B.A. in Writing at Concordia College before completing an M.A. in English Literature/Creative Writing at Kansas State University. He currently lives in the Greater Twin Cities area of Minnesota with his wife Jennifer and four children. Bryn has been teaching for 10 years at secondary and collegiate levels. Outside the classroom, he enjoys tennis, low brass instruments, cooking, hunting, foraging, and a variety of other interests. He is so pleased to offer this first collection for your surprise and delight.

Publication History

"Clear Path" – *Mosaic 51*

"Muscle Memory" – *The Round 8*

"Mouths to Feed" – *Red Earth Review 1*

"Grapefruit" – *Lunch Ticket 3*

"Bandaging" – *Ducts.org 31*

"Orange Thumb" – *Ducts.org 31*

"A Woman Nurses on the Beijing Subway" – *Hawai'i Pacific Review (2014)*

"Decay" – *Flint Hills Review 18*

"Overheard in Leaves" – *Chicago Quarterly Review 18*

"The First Surfer" – *Jet Fuel Review 8*

"I See My Own MRI" – *Jabberwock Review 35.2*

"As Slow as Possible" – *The Turnip Truck(s) 1.1*

"The Unfinished" – *The Turnip Truck(s) 1.1*

"Two Harmonicas" – *The Turnip Truck(s) 1.1*

"Subzero Hunt" – *The Tishman Review 2.1*

"Evening Harvest" – *The Tishman Review 2.1*

"On a Walkthrough of My Wife's Childhood Home" – *Metonym 6*

"My Newborn Gets an IV" – *Ponder Review 1.1*

"Melding" – *The Way to My Heart: An Anthology of Food-Related Romance*

"Pipe, Wood" – *The Maine Review 4.1*

"Young Twins Watch an Accordion" – *3Elements Review 18*

"Ribbon Bound" – *The Remembered Arts Journal (2017)*

"Ingrained" – *Clearing Paths: An Anthology of Verse*

"She Made Us Soup"– *Clearing Paths: An Anthology of Verse*

"My Optometrist Tells Me I Would Have Been a Blacksmith"–
    Clearing Paths: An Anthology of Verse

"The Sky Underground"– *Clearing Paths: An Anthology of Verse*

"Chasing the Burr"– *Clearing Paths: An Anthology of Verse*

"At 5 A.M."– *Clearing Paths: An Anthology of Verse*

$15.00
ISBN 979-8-9863904-3-7
51500>

9 798986 390437

www.ingramcontent.com/pod-product-compliance
Lightning Source LLC
Chambersburg PA
CBHW070727130626
46553CB00005B/2187